Santa Monica Bay
THE FIRST 100 YEARS

A PICTORIAL HISTORY OF
SANTA MONICA, VENICE, OCEAN PARK
PACIFIC PALISADES, TOPANGA & MALIBU

by Fred E. Basten

Pd $12.50 at Phoenix Books, SLO, 21 July 1987

DOUGLAS-WEST PUBLISHERS

LOS ANGELES, CALIFORNIA

To

SANTA MONICA BAY

. . . with love

SECOND PRINTING

Library of Congress Catalogue Card Number 74-83618.
ISBN 0-913264-17-2

Published 1974 by Douglas-West Publishers, Inc.,
   Los Angeles, California.
Printed in the United States by American Yearbook Company.

ILLUSTRATIONS

HOW IT ALL STARTED

While actual development of the Bay Area did not noticeably begin until the founding of Santa Monica in the mid-1870s, the struggle for possession of this valuable coastline land began much earlier when the title to the Bay (and all of California) became vested in the King of Spain with the Spanish occupation in 1769. The occupation was begun by Gaspar de Portola at San Diego and was followed by the establishment in California of presidios, missions and pueblos.

In 1822, California became Mexican territory. Santa Monica, at this time, was still an unoccupied and unclaimed mesa covered with wild grass. There were visitors, however, to the Malibu Rancho, lying northwesterly of Topanga Canyon, which had been granted in 1804 to Jose Bartolome Tapia. Smugglers, too, had discovered the isolated coves and canyons along the coastline.

In 1827, Xavier Alvarado and Antonio Machado were given a provisional grant to "a place called Santa Monica," referring to Santa Monica Canyon and the land that lay between it and Topanga Canyon, extending to the hills in the rear. Machado gave up his interest to Alvarado in 1831 and, when Alvarado died, his sons remained in possession until 1838 when they abandoned "Santa Monica" to Ysidro Reyes and Francisco Marquez.

The year following the Alvarado-Machado grant to "a place called Santa Monica" (1828), Don Francisco Sepulveda, soldier and citizen of that growing inland town, Los Angeles, was given possession of and provisional title to "the place called San Vicente," which included all of the original town of Santa Monica. It faced the ocean, extending from Santa Monica Canyon to what is now Pico Boulevard. Inland, it reached almost to the Westwood region and took in the mountains that overlooked the San Fernando Valley.

The two factions that claimed ownership of the rancho would soon be involved in a lengthy dispute over "Santa Monica." They brought cattle, horses and sheep to their new land and established residences. Sepulveda built an adobe house near San Vicente Springs (now West Los Angeles) while Reyes settled on the bluff of the Huntington Palisades. Later, he moved across the Canyon to a place where his sheep would have better protection from the wolves. Francisco Marquez built farther down in the Canyon.

The grant to Francisco Sepulveda was confirmed by California Governor Alvarado in December, 1839, and with that action the battle began between the Sepulvedas, on the one side, and the Reyes and Marquez families on the other. Both claimed ownership of "Santa Monica."

THE FIRST HOUSE in Santa Monica was built by landowner Ysidro Reyes in 1839 near Seventh Street and Adelaide Drive - close to the spot where Seventh Street now dips into the Canyon. Reyes originally had settled on a bluff of the Huntington Palisades but moved across the Canyon where his sheep would have better protection from marauding animals. Weathered and crumbling, the adobe building was destroyed in 1906.

BY THE LATE 1860s, Santa Monica Canyon was being used as a summer resort by travelers from Los Angeles to escape the heat and dust of the city. The visitors pitched canvas tents, enjoyed the sun and surf, lit scattered bonfires, and held Saturday night dances. Despite the merry-making on their land, the Reyes and Marquez families were very tolerant. Nor did they seem to mind the limited number of establishments that surfaced to cater to the visitors. In 1870, a saloon opened. A year later, a modest hotel. Ads in the Los Angeles papers cried, "A week at the beach will add ten years to your life!" Over the next 20 years the popularity of this hide-away spread, as did its glowing publicity: "After a short drive along Ocean Avenue, the Canyon is reached, with its numerous white tents peeping from the green foliage. The Canyon is so filled with wonders that the mind is thrown into a state of pleasurable surprise and ecstacy when from all sides scenes of enchantment burst upon the vision. Thick clusters of bushes and trees extending a welcome shelter from the hot sun, cool mountain water streams, beds of moss and ferns, shady nooks and tempting lovers' walks. It is all so beautiful, and as you wend your way homeward an impression is felt that only some hours silence alone can satisfy." Santa Monica Canyon was actually the first community - in the summertime, at least - in the Bay Area.

4

The dispute was settled when the Board of Land Commissioners, created in 1851 to investigate and pass upon land titles in California, ruled that Sepulveda would receive "Rancho San Vicente y Santa Monica" with 30,000 acres. To Reyes and Marquez went "Boca de Santa Monica" with 6,600 acres.

In the late 1860's, Santa Monica Canyon was discovered as a summer camping grounds by visitors from Los Angeles. The Reyes and Marquez families were very tolerant of the "intruders." On the mesa itself, site of the unborn town of Santa Monica, a trail crossed the grass-covered prairie to the foot of what is now Colorado Avenue. Colonel R.S. Baker, a cattleman who had come to San Francisco from Rhode Island, made a trip to the area in 1872. He looked over the flat expanse and, deciding it would make a good sheep ranch, went to the Sepulveda heirs and paid them $55,000 for their rancho. Later, he bought part of the Reyes-Marquez property adjoining on the northwest, plus a portion of Rancho La Ballona adjoining San Vicente on the southeast.

Senator John Percival Jones of Nevada, a Comstock millionaire, appeared on the scene in 1874 and bought three-fourths interest in Colonel Baker's ranch for $162,500. Together they planned a railroad, a wharf and a town.

On July 10, 1875, a map of "Santa Monica" was recorded in the office of the County Recorder in Los Angeles. The townsite fronted on the ocean and was bounded on the northwest by Montana Avenue, on the southeast by Railroad Avenue (now Colorado) and on the northeast by 26th Street. The Los Angeles papers were divided on their new neighbor. One derisively labeled the town "Jonesville" and began attacking it as a deliberate attempt to build a rival city and destroy Los Angeles. Another rallied to Santa Monica's defense and said that by securing the trade of the Inyo silver mines (which Senator Jones owned) and the resulting harbor activity, it would be Los Angeles' savior. A few days later a much-advertised first sale of lots was held from an auctioneer's stand located near the foot of what is now Wilshire Boulevard. On hand were over 150 people who arrived by steamer from San Francisco, plus nearly 2,000 others, most of whom traveled by stages, wagons and buggies from Los Angeles. The auctioneer was Thomas Fitch, former California Congressman and leading orator on the Pacific coast. He sold the first lot, the northeast corner of Ocean Avenue and Utah (now Broadway), for $510 to a gentleman who also bought four others, all on Ocean Avenue, for $300 each. Over $40,000 worth of Jones' lots were sold the first day. The next day, $43,000 was counted in sales.

Within nine months, Santa Monica had 1,000 people, 160 houses and half as many tents. Tracks for the Los Angeles & Independence Railroad, sponsored by Senator Jones, had been laid from the ocean to Los Angeles and a wharf was in operation. That same year saw a school district organized, a church established, the beginnings of a public library, a bathhouse, a hotel and a newspaper.

The boom had started. Santa Monica, and the Bay Area, was on its way.

THE SENATOR AND HIS LADY

John P. Jones, founder of Santa Monica, was born in England, raised in Ohio, and was equally at home in the mines of Virginia City or addressing a roomful of politicians as Senator from Nevada. In Washington, where he was a widower (his first wife died shortly after their marriage), he was described as dynamic, fearless, extremely personable and "the catch of the capital." His limited high school education served to trigger his interests rather than deter them. In time, he became a distinguished orator (it is said he had the faculty of making columns of figures sound as fascinating as a novel), an avid student of men and books, a patron of arts and letters, and one of the most respected legislators and statesmen of his time—as well as one of the wealthiest. In spite of his fortune, he reportedly cared little for money. Perhaps that is why he was so generous in his gifts to the city he founded and to his adopted country. Colonel Baker's widow, Arcadia, and Senator Jones (who owned three-quarters share of all holdings) donated the parkland at Lincoln and Wilshire Boulevards, innumerable church sites, various public school grounds, the strip of land bordering Ocean Avenue now known as Palisades Park, and 640 acres to the government for the establishment of a National Military Home (the Veteran's Administration) at Sawtelle.

Georgina Sullivan Jones, the Senator's second wife, was the daughter of the Hon. Eugene L. Sullivan, collector of the Port of San Francisco. Tabloids reported that she presided over their Santa Monica home, Miramar, "in a warm, refined and gracious manner, adding much to the charm of the stately residence." Three daughters (Alice, Marion and Georgina) were born to this marriage.

'SHOO FLY' PIER, Santa Monica's first, was a dismal loading point for La Brea tar shipments even in its prime. Eventually, it was partially destroyed by fire and the remaining portions had to be leveled. It was at "Shoo Fly" landing that Senator Jones envisioned Santa Monica as an important world port. Barely visible in this photo are horseback riders in the surf.

SANTA MONICA'S FIRST wharf was completed in April, 1875. Built by the Jones and Baker interests, the wharf was located at "Shoo Fly" landing - just south of today's Municipal Pier at the foot of Colorado Avenue. It was from this spot that steamers from San Francisco arrived with passengers for the first land sale. Condemned by the Southern Pacific in 1878, the wharf was in operation only three years.

SANTA MONICA IN 1876, one year after its founding. As "gateway to the Inyo silver mines," being on the proposed route of Senator Jones' Los Angeles & Independence Railroad, the town had attracted a population of 1,000 people. Rows of buildings lined Ocean Avenue, Second and Third Streets for several blocks north of the tracks and, for a time, it looked like the typical frontier mining town with false fronts, board walks and dirt streets. Cattle and stray horses roamed at will eating the tender, young leaves of newly planted trees - and gun-toting residents found great sport in shooting at the circling sea gulls. (The illustration was drawn by an unidentified artist shortly after Santa Monica was founded. Although several key buildings were incorrectly located, historians agree that, on the whole, it is a very accurate representation of the Bay at the time.)

IN 1876, Santa Monica boasted 160 homes - and half as many tents.

THE FIRST 'RESORT DEVELOPMENT' on Santa Monica beach was the Santa Monica Bath House. Built in 1877, it featured hot steam baths, a plunge and facilities for salt water bathing. The bath house was reached by a series of steps, 99 in all, leading from the palisades to the sand. This scene was taken about 1884.

11

COLLAPSE...AND RECOVERY

The crash in Comstock mining securities in the late '70s took a heavy toll on Senator Jones' fortune. Although he later recouped, he had to abandon his Los Angeles & Independence Railroad (once called the "biggest little railroad in the United States") to rival magnate Collis P. Huntington who purchased the line for Southern Pacific. In 1878, the final blow fell: Southern Pacific condemned and partially dismantled the Santa Monica wharf. The collapse of mining securities, the loss of the railroad and wharf left the town without hope. Santa Monica's population dwindled to 350 people. Land sales fell off abruptly. Prices of unimproved land in the county dropped from a high of $100 per acre to a new low of $30.

Increasing activity "down the street," however, was soon to create an unexpected upswing. Searching for a more convenient terminal near Los Angeles, the Santa Fe Railroad secured a right-of-way between the bustling inland community and the mouth of Ballona Creek, just four miles south of Santa Monica. The town of La Ballona was laid out on paper and an improvement company began dredging a harbor big enough to "float the fleets of the world." By the spring of 1887, two wharves had been built into the surf and a channel was being dug between the ocean and the large inland lagoon. From its connection in Los Angeles, the Santa Fe began laying track toward the coast. Along the way several towns, including Palms, were born. In August of '87 the first train reached La Ballona.

While the Los Angeles & Independence Railroad had failed to make Santa Monica a transcontinental outlet, the Santa Fe was accomplishing the job for another town at its very door. Once again, Santa Monica property values began increasing. Jones and Baker were now selling lots near the beach in their Ocean Spray tract (south Santa Monica) and inland as far as 20th Street - and prices were climbing rapidly. New business buildings, many of them brick, were rising along Second, Third and Fourth Streets. Elaborate residences, a number in the gingerbread style of the day, appeared on Ocean Avenue and the residential streets surrounding downtown. The boom of '87 was transforming the face of Santa Monica.

J.W. Scott, the energetic proprietor of the Santa Monica Hotel (the city's first hotel), had reaped enough out of the revival to launch a resort on the south side of town where, on the crown of the palisades, he built the grand Arcadia Hotel.

SANTA MONICA BEACH and palisades (looking north from a point opposite where Wilshire Boulevard ends today), 1886. Then, as today, the bluff ranged from 80'-125' high over its two mile length.

The Arcadia Hotel, on Ocean Avenue between Railroad Avenue (now Colorado) and Front (now Pico), was for many years one of the most distinguished hotels on the Pacific coast - and a true Santa Monica landmark, being the city's first skyline building. Opened in late 1887, it was named for Arcadia Bandini Baker, wife of Colonel Robert Baker, "grandfather" of Santa Monica. Tabloids praised the Arcadia more than any other local hostelry of the period. Reported one, in 1893: "The Arcadia Hotel is a first-class, high-grade resort, built upon the finest hotel site on the coast. To the many thousands of patrons of the past, this famous resort has afforded seaside pleasures before unknown and today stands without peer for furnishing true, modernized life at the seashore. In the rear of the house, observatory verandas, replete with shady nooks, afford delicious after-meal lounging places. Here may be admired at one's ease the rolling ocean, while below extending on either side a distance of several miles, is a sandy beach with thousands of pleasure seekers strolling along, and many hundreds more disporting themselves among the breakers. That this hotel was built for the comfort of the guests is plainly seen by looking over the premises. On the first floor, across from the front entrance, is a well arranged reception parlor and hotel office in one. On the left is the dining room, which comfortably seats 200 guests. On the right a large hall leads to the sitting room and parlor, also the writing, ladies' billiard and reading rooms. Directly opposite the main entrance is the elevator which runs to the floors above and two below where the ballroom, a conservatory and other places of accommodation are to be found. On the basement floor access to the beach is made, where hot salt water baths may be enjoyed by those who cannot stand the cold water. The house is furnished throughout with gas and electric light, hot and cold water, bath rooms, and all the modern improvements which conduce to the comfort of guests. In short, we take great pleasure in recommending the Arcadia Hotel to all pleasure seekers and others who visit Santa Monica."

MAIN ENTRANCE to the Arcadia Hotel on Ocean Avenue, ca 1889.

PIER NEAR THE ARCADIA HOTEL was simply for the enjoyments of guests and visitors who wanted to stroll over the surf or watch the changing sky.

THE ARCADIA HOTEL, ocean side, ca 1893.

SANTA MONICA CANYON'S first bath house was owned by Pascual Marquez, son of Francisco Marquez, original owner of the land grant. It was located on the beach against the side of the palisade, just north of the incline where Chautauqua Boulevard is today. The horse-drawn wagon was the Santa Monica Canyon stage, started by a Los Angeles liveryman to take Sunday excursionists to the shore. The stage's route is now Washington Boulevard, the earliest road between Los Angeles and Santa Monica.

18

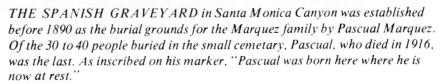

THE SPANISH GRAVEYARD in Santa Monica Canyon was established before 1890 as the burial grounds for the Marquez family by Pascual Marquez. Of the 30 to 40 people buried in the small cemetary, Pascual, who died in 1916, was the last. As inscribed on his marker. "Pascual was born here where he is now at rest."

SANTA MONICA BEACH, 1887. For several years, this unused strip of ocean front attracted a group of squatters who erected makeshift shanties on the sand. The brief period was known as the "beach shack era." The steepled building beyond the pier is the Arcadia Hotel. Note man sitting on bench at edge of palisade (far left).

20

THE MAN FROM MASSACHUSETTES

In 1887, Frederick Hastings Rindge, member of a wealthy Massachusettes family, brought his bride, Rhoda May Knight, to live in Los Angeles. That same year he purchased the Malibu rancho, a Spanish grant. He soon added other lands until his holdings covered 25 miles of coast, canyons, mesas and mountain ridges. Four years later, the Rindges moved to their newly completed family home on Ocean Avenue in Santa Monica.

Frederick Rindge was of Puritan stock and when he came to California he carried with him the beliefs of Evangelism. His influence on the moral and religious history of Santa Monica was strong. He built the Methodist Church at Arizona and Fourth Street and was a founder of the Santa Monica branch YMCA that made its home in Ocean Park. His genius and leadership extended beyond local boundaries, as well. Rindge helped to found Union Oil Company, Southern California Edison Company, and the life insurance firm that became Pacific Mutual. He was also president of the Harvard Club of Los Angeles from its inception until his death, at age 48, in 1905.

THE RINDGE RANCH HOUSE on Laudamus Hill (now site of Serra Retreat) in Malibu. It was destroyed by fire in 1903.

THE RINDGE FAMILY HOME at 454 Ocean Avenue in Santa Monica. Ca 1895.

'PORT OF LOS ANGELES'

As early as January, 1888, there were signs that the "Great Boom of '87" was weakening. News from La Ballona was that the Santa Fe might drop the harbor project, finding it "impractical." Not much later, the dredging was halted and the paper town of Ballona was left unbuilt. Throughout the area, land values plummeted and mammoth hotels under construction were abandoned. Even many of the established hotels and resorts were forced to close for lack of business - among them the elegant Arcadia.

It was left to Collis P. Huntington to create the next boom by announcing plans to build a giant wharf just north of Santa Monica, regaining for the town the shipping and trade that had been lost earlier.

In 1891, a new wharf was constructed by Huntington for Southern Pacific at the mouth of Potrero Canyon. He named the site "Port of Los Angeles" but residents knew it as the "Long Wharf." Snaking 4,700 feet into the ocean, it was the largest and longest wharf in the world, incorporating two sets of railroad tracks (one standard width, the other narrow gauge) that branched into seven tracks at the 130-foot-wide seaward end. There, a series of coal bunkers, a warehouse (with a storage capacity for 8,200 tons), a depot and unloading facilities were located. The docking area could accommodate three coal ships at once and more could be worked if necessary. Too, the Pacific Coast Steamship Company made "Port of Los Angeles" a regular stop, running steamers from San Francisco. For the traveler, a baggage room and restaurant had been constructed. There was also a special area set aside for sailors and fishermen with a stairway leading down to a platform and boathouse near the water level.

THE LONG WHARF from Huntington Palisades, 1894. In the distance, a steamer rides the horizon line off Point Dume.

'PORT OF LOS ANGELES'...

The Long Wharf had rekindled the old dream of creating a major seaport in Santa Monica Bay, along with creating a new surge of activity within Santa Monica. Business was booming. Hotels and resorts were thriving. And the Arcadia reopened with great fanfare. But the local citizens were not alone in wanting the world's shipping trade and it wasn't long before a "harbor war" erupted between Santa Monica and San Pedro. Santa Monica forces claimed that their city was closer to Los Angeles, the commercial and railroad center of Southern California, that its bay (by virtue of its shape, depth of water and topography) was more suitable for a deep sea harbor, that materials for construction of a huge breakwater (one measuring nearly two miles long was planned for the Bay just off of Santa Monica Canyon) were nearer and, therefore, would be less expensive, and so on. Advocates of San Pedro claimed the reverse

continued . . . page 32

26

TERMINAL SECTION of the Long Wharf, 1893. Coal bunkers are stationed on pier left, with the depot and large warehouse on the right. The wharf also had provisions for travelers arriving by steamer. When the first steamer docked in May, 1893, more than 1,000 local citizens rode Southern Pacific cars up the line to welcome the group. While the Santa Monica town band played, residents swarmed aboard ship and decked it with home grown flowers.

27

THE LONG WHARF at Potrero Canyon, 1892.

LOOKING SHOREWARD from near the end of the Long Wharf, 1893. The two-track portion leading to land was 3,100 feet long and 28 feet wide, flaring out at the docking area for an additional 1,600 feet to a maximum width of 130 feet. On shore, between Potrero Canyon (left) and Santa Monica Canyon (right) is the escarpment of the Huntington Palisades.

'PORT OF LOS ANGELES' from the mouth of Potrero Canyon, 1893. Line of empty coal cars waits to be loaded at bunkers on wharf's end where coal, shipped from Vancouver Island, was stored for Southern Pacific. Note turntable for engines (lower right).

'PORT OF LOS ANGELES'...

was true on all counts. The controversy raged until 1897 when a decision favoring San Pedro was announced. Work on the new harbor began in 1899.

With the loss of shipping trade, the Long Wharf became little more than a tourist attraction. In 1916, it was reduced to half-size and made into a fishing pier for residents and visitors. The remaining portion was removed entirely in 1921.

The decision favoring San Pedro was a turning point in the destiny of Santa Monica Bay. Disappointed residents were unaware that their coastline would soon be transformed into one of the most popular resort areas in the world.

TODAY, all that remains of the Long Wharf is a portion of its rocky foundation.

RAILROAD TRACKS parallel the shore on their way to the Long Wharf, 1894 - now the route of Pacific Coast Highway (U.S. 101).

32

IN 1892, Santa Monica's resident population was only 2,000 but tourists more than doubled the figure. "People from Los Angeles are overrunning the beach both summer and winter," one newspaper reported. By the early 1970s, over 16 million people a year flocked to Santa Monica's shoreline.

ARCH ROCK, located on the beach just south of Topanga Canyon, was one of the Bay Area's most popular natural wonders. The arch was so wide that, when the tide was low, horse drawn wagons could pass through the opening. Old-time residents are at a loss to explain what happened to Arch Rock. "It just disappeared," they say. Ca 1890.

35

LAYING SIDEWALKS along Oregon Street (now Santa Monica Boulevard), 1890. Over the next few years, Santa Monica became noted for its well-developed roads. Several of the main streets were curbed and paved while others were oiled. The system was copied by many other communities. (Left) Same street today. Bay Cities Building, with its famous clock tower, was Santa Monica's first "skyscraper." It opened in March, 1929.

BANK OF SANTA MONICA, the city's first bank, occupied what was described as "an elegant building on the southeast corner of Oregon and Third Streets. The quarters are roomy and well lighted, the office fixtures and furnishings being modern extend to patrons every facility while transacting business." In 1893, the Bank was capitalized for $50,000 and was an active factor in promoting Santa Monica's interests. The second floor of the building housed the city's first library.

With the electric line running eastward down Oregon Street, new subdivisions opened all the way from Santa Monica to Sawtelle. These and other developments, as well as residential growth, were responsible for downtown Santa Monica's new-found metropolitan spirit.

VIEW NORTH FROM THE ARCADIA HOTEL with the Long Wharf in the distance, ca 1893. Stairway connected buildings in foreground are part of a complex that comprised the Santa Monica Pavilion Restaurant. According to a pamphlet, dated 1893: "This famous family resort has, besides the fine dining room which overlooks the beach and ocean, a number of private dining rooms for parties. Three hundred guests may be seated at one time in the Pavilion and, on a recent Fourth of July, over 1,500 people were dined between the hours of noon and 2:00 pm. No one should fail to visit the Pavilion Restaurant and while partaking of the good things there to be found, enjoy the beautiful sea scenery and inhale the appetizing ozone." (Just beyond the Pavilion, note the curve of the railroad tracks as it cuts into the break between the palisades. Today, that same curve is the route of Pacific Coast Highway as it passes through McClure Tunnel leading to the entrance of the eastbound Santa Monica Freeway.) In 1893, virtually all of Santa Monica was lighted by electricity.

BIRDSEYE VIEW NORTH from the Arcadia Hotel, 1892, showing depot for incoming trains and trolleys. Ocean Avenue bridge crossed over tracks where today's bridge tops McClure Tunnel. Ferris wheel (upper left center) was on the grounds of the original Santa Monica Hotel. A portion of the Pavilion Restaurant is shown at left.

ANOTHER VIEW from the Arcadia Hotel, four years later. Train depot, shown in earlier photo, is dark building in center. Railroad tracks followed essentially the same route as today's Colorado Avenue, then called Railroad Avenue.

MIRAMAR, the home of Senator John P. Jones, founder of Santa Monica, ca 1895. Construction on the estate, located on the grounds of the hotel that now bears its name, began in 1887 and was completed two years later at a cost of $40,000. "Miramar, with its 17 bedrooms, was enormous," recalls Dorothy Jones Boden, the Senator's granddaughter. "He wanted to make sure he had ample room for his mother and her relatives from Cleveland. He loved having everyone with him." Today, the only reminder of Miramar is the giant Moreton fig tree. Says Mrs. Boden, "Gone are the orchards, the rose arbors, the tennis court, chicken houses and stables, and the barn. Why, we had livestock right on the property. In those days, the corner of Ocean and California was a cow pasture."

42

CHRISTMAS PARTY at Miramar, 1897. The Senator's young relations, and their guests, gather around the tree during a holiday get-together. Family members are (left of tree): Hal Gorham, Gregory Jones, Mrs. Roy Jones and Dorothy Jones.

THE ROY JONES FAMILY HOME, ca 1895.
It is still standing in the 1000 block on Ocean
Avenue, one block away from the site of his
father's estate, Miramar.

ONE OF THE BEST KNOWN NAMES in early Santa Monica
was George Boehme. Arriving from the east in 1875, he soon
became a leading force in the city. Aside from operating his own
hardware store, which featured everything from stoves and small
kitchen furnishings to plumbing and fishing equipment, Boehme
financed and constructed the Boehme Block, Laurence House,
Boehme Villa and other buildings. He served on the Board of
School Trustees from 1877 to 1880 and was elected
town Treasurer in 1892.

INTERIOR of George Boehme's hardward store, 1893.

SANTA MONICA BEACH and palisades (looking north from near today's Broadway), ca 1895. Note train heading for the Long Wharf, horse on the beach and "99 steps."

'PEARL OF THE PACIFIC'

Pacific Electric's "Balloon Route," which brought hordes of summer beach goers to Santa Monica, helped tide the low period that followed San Pedro's victory in the harbor war. It was the beginning of a constant, unrefined ballyhoo campaign that sparked the growth of the coastal cities. Ads blazed with new catch phrases: "The Zenith City By The Sunset Sea" ... "Where Summer Spends The Year" ... "The Pearl of the Pacific" ... "The Gem By The Sea" ... "Mountain Guarded" ... "Ocean Washed" ... "Sun Kissed." No argument was overlooked to drive home the area's matchless climate. Papers reported, "The thermometer has very little to do at Santa Monica other than registering daily the

continued ...

AD FROM 1902
(Morocco Junction is now Beverly Hills)

'PEARL OF THE PACIFIC'...

same old story" and openly called the city a "terrestrial paradise where life was pleasant, languid and carefree." As a clinching attraction for the lonely, it was noted that "the glistening sands keep no record of the innocent flirtations of those who indulge in this harmless pastime."

The effect of the campaign was remarkable. Inlanders streamed to the beach and each summer the hotels, cottages and boarding houses were filled to capacity. Rivalry with Long Beach and Redondo was intense. When a Long Beach paper claimed that 6,000 tourists jammed its city's beaches one Fourth of July, a Santa Monica resident responded, "I don't doubt it ... the overflow from our beaches had to go some place."

By 1900, it was becoming obvious that the promotional selling job was beginning to have a residual effect. Tourists had seen the advantage of living at the beach and discovered that the 35 minute running time of the electric railway permitted them to live on the coast and work in Los Angeles. Those who came for their health found that the climate alone was enough to get them to stay. Here was the opportunity for a long awaited revival.

Beginning in 1901, real estate values began to climb once more. Leading the new awakening was an ambitious young man in search of an outlet for his talent as an organizer and promoter, Abbot Kinney.

OPENING DAY (April 1, 1896) of Pacific Electric's trolley excursions from Los Angeles to the beach attracted a large number of pleasure seekers - but nothing like what was to come. During the summer, the trains ran almost continually. And the crowds were said to be so thick they seemed to pour out of the cars. The electric train opened a new era of growth for the resort cities.

MAIN PLUNGE at the North Beach Bath House, ca 1900. The sideline gallery was often filled with visitors watching the swimmers at play.

NORTH BEACH BATH HOUSE, on the strand just north of the Santa Monica fishing pier, was for many years without rival as the area's favorite resort facility. Built about 1893, it was said to have "every improvement that tends to a bather's comfort." A special feature, and one taken advantage of by many thousands annually, was the hot salt water bath. For the "weak and exhausted," this form of bathing was highly recommended by the medical profession as both "refreshing and strengthening." The admission fee of twenty-five cents was evidently reasonable as the baths were constantly occupied. Attendants, on duty at all times, were described as attentive and courteous. A portion of the building also housed the new Pavilion Restaurant, shops and a bowling pavilion. In 1902, an auditorium was built nearby making North Beach the outstanding beach center for tourists, holiday crowds and "hometown" parties.

51

PACIFIC GARDEN, a favorite lunch stop and gathering place, dominated Ocean Avenue between Utah (now Broadway) and Railroad Avenue (Colorado) at the turn of the century. Said an early pamphlet, "To those who wish a quiet place to eat their lunch, and be protected from the mid-day sun, Pacific Garden is recommended. The refreshment hall is large and the adjoining garden contains seats for many hundreds of people. Every visitor will find everything served promptly and with the best of taste."

ANOTHER VIEW of the coastline from the tower of the Arcadia Hotel, ca 1895. The North Beach Bath House, with its pedistrian overpass from the palisade, was only recently completed. Pacific Garden, popular tourist stop, is seen on Ocean Avenue (far right).

POINT DUME in Malibu, ca 1898. It was somewhere near this point on October 8, 1542, that Juan Cabrillo's high-decked Spanish galleon dropped anchor to survey the landscape of the area. His diary recorded, "A good port; and the country is good with many valleys and plains and trees." The land was also inhabited, as Cabrillo discovered from the many columns of smoke rising from Indian camps or signal fires. His men named the coastline the "Bay of Smokes."

Point Dume, which frames Santa Monica Bay on the west, was named by George Vancouver, an English explorer. Commissioned by King George III to explore California's coastline, Vancouver reached the Malibu area during 1782. Traveling farther up the coast, he stopped at Mission San Buena Ventura where he met Father Francisco Dumetz. Vancouver named Point Dume after Father Dumetz. (The dome on the point was originally rounded, as shown. In later years, it was "shaved" or flattened for possible building development.)

THE LONG WHARF and the beach at Santa Monica Canyon from Santa Monica's Inspiration Point, 1899.

55

THE CORNER BLOCKS

"Class," in the early days, was having a corner business building and naming it your "block." Here are two from 1900: the Whitworth Block, Second Street and Utah (now Broadway) and the Keller Block, Third Street and Utah. On the upper floors of the Keller Block was the 45-room Jackson Hotel, described in a publication of that era as "tastefully furnished and supplied with everything necessary for the accommodation of guests. Each room is connected with the office by an electric bell for calling guests in the morning, thus doing away with the old system of knocking on doors and awaking those who do not have to arise until late." The Jackson's dining table was a distinctive feature of the hotel - and reportedly was abundantly supplied with everything the markets of the day could afford. Rooms at the Jackson went for $2.00 per day, with special rates for families. The Keller Block, minus its fortress-like roof ornamentation, is still standing.

The Whitworth Block

The Keller Block

Dining Room,
JACKSON HOTEL

57

LOOKING NORTH along Ocean Avenue from Nevada Avenue (now Wilshire Boulevard), ca 1900. Hitching posts in front of most homes and carriage steps at the curb were considered great conveniences. The stand of eucalyptus trees lining the street was a gift to the city from J.W. Scott, builder of the Arcadia Hotel. (Inset) Ocean Avenue today, looking north past Wilshire.

58

INTERSECTION of Arizona Avenue and Second Street, ca 1900. (Inset) Same view today.

IN 1900, OCEAN VIEW HOUSE was so far out of town it was practically a retreat. Located at the northerly end of Ocean Avenue (near Georgina), it was one of the most picturesque of Santa Monica's early resort hotels.

SANTA MONICA'S FIRST CAMERA OBSCURA

was installed in Linda Vista Park (renamed Palisades Park during the '20s)

about 1901 and was located at the foot of

Oregon Avenue (now Santa Monica Boulevard).

*LORING'S LUNCH ROOM at the shore end (north side) of Santa Monica Pier opened in 1902 and was
a landmark for years. Here, "Bake" Loring and his family pose beside their profitable establishment.*

LINCOLN SCHOOL on Arizona Avenue, ca 1902.

SANTA MONICA
MERCHANTS

Saxman & Tegner Grocers, 256 3rd St.

Santa Monica Steam Laundry, corner 8th & Railroad Ave.

1902

Sues' Ice Cream & Confectionary, N.E. corner 2nd & Utah

M.F. Volkman, Druggist, 213 3rd St.

Crosier's Real Estate, 2nd & Utah

Montgomery's, 231-233 3rd St.

THE PAVILION in Santa Monica Canyon was built primarily as a "fun stop" for the many thousands of people who took the popular Southern Pacific excursions to the coast. The huge building was particularly noted for its dance hall and orchestra. Ca 1902. (The Pavilion had no connection with the Pavilion Restaurant at North Beach in Santa Monica.)

THE PAVILION'S *cavernous dining room could seat over 300 people.*

IN 1903, A NEW CITY HALL was built in Santa Monica at the northwest corner of Fourth Street and Oregon Avenue (Santa Monica Boulevard). During this period telephones were installed in town.

VILLAGE ON THE SANDS

Ocean Park was Abbot Kinney's first real estate development on Santa Monica Bay. Concentrating on providing resort facilities and vacation housing along the beach, he and his partners constructed a small community in less than five years on land that was formerly sandy waste. In 1901, Ocean Park was a village of 200 cottages with a post office, stores, a pleasure pier (extending 1,250 feet into the ocean), an auditorium, a race track and a casino. The development of Ocean Park coincided with a major influx of newcomers from the midwestern states and, at the same time, a boom in home construction. When the town was incorporated in 1904, there was every indication of rapid growth as a year-round residential area as well as a resort. Despite the immediate success of this venture, Kinney was not satisfied. Being a romantic, he began to concentrate on his dream city, the "Venice of America."

LOOKING MORE LIKE A MOVIE SET, the Ocean Park Bath House was one of the most talked about buildings of its day - and a great draw for the beach area. The lavish indoor plunge (heated for those who didn't take to cooler ocean swimming) was built by A.R. Fraser, who earlier had been a partner with Abbot Kinney and others in the Ocean Park Improvement Company. The bath house is shown here just before completion in 1905.

GATEWAY to the Ocean Park
Pier, ca 1905. This promenade
of casinos, cafes and game
parlors eventually became Pier
Avenue. View looking east.

OCEAN PARK'S FIRST beach houses along the boardwalk, ca 1900. The small white building, just below the crest of the hill (left center) is the original Washington School, located at Fourth Street and Ashland.

CARNATION FIELDS in Ocean Park, 1899. A single acre of this experimental garden produced 35,000 carnation blossoms in one season and the carpet of color was one of the advertised tourist attractions on the Santa Fe's line from Los Angeles to Ocean Park. The oldest structures still standing in the area are cottages built in the 1890s when these gardens were established - small frame houses with Victorian ornamentation located on the "Carnation Tract" between Rose and Sunset Avenues, Washington Boulevard and Fourth Street.

OCEAN PARK CASINO, 1902. It was considered "the" place for tennis and teas.

THE BATTLE OF MALIBU

In 1904, the Southern Pacific Railroad planned to institute condemnation proceedings to get a right-of-way through the privately owned Malibu rancho, wanting to link their tracks which ended in Santa Monica on the east and in Santa Barbara on the west. Owner of the rancho, Frederick Hastings Rindge, found that he could prevent the railroad from going through his land by building his own 20-mile narrow-gauge railroad along the coastline. It began at Las Flores Canyon and extended on up the coast, climbing bluffs and leaping canyons past Point Dume, where it dropped down through a cut in the escarpment. From there a low bridge carried the rails over the slough (which usually backed up at Zuma beach) to the shore, following the coastline until it reached the Ventura County line. The railroad was incorporated as the "Hueneme, Malibu and Port Los Angeles Railroad." When Rindge died in 1905, he reportedly advised his wife, May, to protect their lands from intruders. For 17 years, starting in 1908, Mrs. Rindge waged a long and bitter battle with County and State officials who were attempting to acquire a right-of-way through the rancho for a coastal road. She erected high fences and hired armed riders to keep out trespassers and surveying parties. Ultimately, she spent a fortune in attorney's fees, carrying four legal actions to the State Supreme Court and two to the United States Supreme Court. In 1925, the Court gave the State of California a right-of-way for a highway and in 1928 the Roosevelt Highway - now U.S. 101 - was completed and opened to traffic.

RINDGE'S RAILROAD cuts across Ramirez Canyon as cattle graze on the foothills, ca 1906.

DIGGING THE VENICE CANALS in 1904. View east from present post office at Kinney Plaza.

RENAISSANCE IN VENICE

Actual development in the Venice area began in 1892 when Abbot Kinney, world-traveled connoisseur of art and scenic beauty (and wealthy manufacturer of Sweet Caporal cigarettes), induced the Santa Fe Railroad to extend its tracks northward from Port Ballona, the "dream harbor" that was abandoned in the mid-1880's. Like many other literary men of the time, Kinney was convinced that an American renaissance would rise spontaneously in Los Angeles through the inspiration given by the gentle climate and magnificent natural setting to the vigorous people attracted from the east and midwest. He wanted to design a beach com-

munity that would be worthy of such a future - an environment that would foster a cultural awakening. Capitalizing on the similarities between his land and that of Venice, Italy, Kinney actively began in 1900 to build the "Venice of America." He first commissioned architects Norman F. Marsh and C.H. Russell to design the project. He then began negotiations with Henry E.

Huntington's newly organized Pacific Electric Company to assure transportation to the site. Huntington constructed the Lagoon Line south from Santa Monica in 1901 and the following year began grading an entirely new route, the Venice Short Line, directly from downtown Los Angeles. Construction of canals, streets and other capital improvements began in early 1904. While in progress, Kinney personally persuaded merchants, hotel men and restaurateurs to build facilities with fronts, at least, in the architectural style of the Venetian Renaissance. All of his exhuberance and haste, however, probably led to a number of engineering mistakes, the canal system certainly being the worst. The canals were excavated to a depth of only four feet, the dirt being mounded at the sides by horse-drawn scoop shovels without compaction. Little remedial work was done on the canal floors and the whole project was rushed through during a single summer. The tidal action which, Kinney knew, kept the canals of old Venice wholesome, could not maintain circulation through the 16 miles of uniformly shallow ditches open to the sea through only one narrow water gate. By 1912, the State Board of Health had served notice that the canals were a menace to public health. No action to close them, however, was taken until Venice's annexation to Los Angeles in 1925. Two years later, the canals of Abbot Kinney's original design were filled and paved as streets, leaving only the grid comprising Carrol, Linnie, Howland and Sherman, between Grand and Eastern Canals, as waterways.

THE VENICE BATH HOUSE shortly before opening, 1904. Located on the corner of Main Street and Windward Avenue (now the site of a bank), the building was designed to accommodate over 5,000 bathers. In later years, it served as a high school for the area. The canals, finished only a short time in the photo, had not yet been landscaped.

LOOKING WEST across Venice's Main Lagoon (now the traffic circle) toward the concessions area, 1908. The fanciest of all shoreline developments, Venice was an enormous fantasy. As one old-timer recalls, "Pale imitation it may have been but the air of constant excitement was genuine . . . and if the pleasures it afforded were too innocent to match a landscape deliberately suggestive of the sinister delights of the Renaissance, they were nonetheless satisfying. Venice was a collection of gorgeous excesses. Potted palms and pennants lined the streets in constant celebration - of what I was never sure - and the architecture was the grandest . . . an intricate blend of Italian columns, porticos and ballastrades, only slightly marred by the presence of guess-your-weight machines."

*BOATING ALONG ALDEBARAN CANAL (now Market Street) in Venice, ca 1909.
According to an early Chamber of Commerce report, "At night the canals are lighted by
myriads of varicolored electric globes which look like gigantic jewels when reflected in the
limpid waters of the street-wide canals." To add romance and authenticity to the scene, Abbot
Kinney imported two dozen gondoliers from old Venice, complete with black, silver-prowed
gondolas and repertoires of Italian songs. (Right) Canal scene today.*

FINISHING TOUCHES go on the St. Mark Hotel just before its opening, ca 1905. The hotel, at Windward and Ocean Front Walk, was one of Venice's most distinguished and, in later years, vied with the nearby Waldorf as "the" place to stay. Its guestlist included such famous names as Douglas Fairbanks and Rudolph Valentino. (Inset) Portions of the St. Mark's decorative colonnade are still standing and may be seen on a stroll down Ocean Front.

A NEW RESPECTABILITY

With Ocean Park and Venice taking up the "carnival spirit," Santa Monica began emphasizing ease of living, the quiet home life, pleasant and cultural surroundings, and finally decided that its true future was in making the most of its natural assets. But while it had unparalled climate and scenery, it also had a reputation for being a tough town. One irate citizen wrote to a local paper saying, "Passengers on the Balloon Route should be blindfolded while passing through Santa Monica." The town was wide open. Saloons flourished. Park benches and street corners were "strewn with unsavory characters."

The reform was initiated by the influencial Frederick Hastings Rindge. He led the fight to close Santa Monica's saloons, offering to personally pay the money the city would lose in license fees . . . and won.

By the time the building boom began to subside in 1906 (the Palisades tract - the area between Montana Avenue and Adelaide Drive - was opened just the year before), Santa Monica had thrown off its frontier appearance. No longer did it cater to beach crowds who had abandoned it in favor of Ocean Park and Venice. Once again the Arcadia Hotel had closed, this time to convert to a private school. As one observer noted, "Santa Monica has no hotel, no first-class restaurant, and offers few attractions for the transcient. But it draws a constantly increasing number of permanent residents of the better class." Suddenly, Santa Monica began to rival Pasadena as the "home city" for Southern Californians. Between 1900 and 1905, population jumped from 3,057 to 7,208.

Residence of N.R. Folsom, 407 Arizona Ave.

Residence of W.H. Perry, 250 Ocean Ave.

Residence of R.R. Tanner, 144 4th St.

Residence of J.G. Knesel, 448 2nd St.

Residence of H.W. Keller, 310 Ocean Ave.

Residence of T.H. Dudley, 513 4th St.

Residence of Miss E. Wright, 448 3rd St.

Residence of J. Haverwaas, 339 3rd St.

83

1902

Christian Church, 5th St.

Methodist Church, 4th & Ariz

First Church of Christ (Scientist), Oregon Ave.

Catholic Church, 3rd St.

Presbyterian Chu

84

& Arizona

Academy of the Holy Names, 3rd & Arizona

85

SANTA MONICA Fire House & Combination Wagon, 1902.

OCEAN PARK Fire House & Hose Cart, 1902.

J.R. Le Berge's Union Stables

G.G. Bundy's Santa Monica Stables

TWO OF SANTA MONICA'S finest liveries, 1902. Union Stables was located at 128 Second Street; Santa Monica Stables at 314 Utah (Broadway). Both offered first-class "equipage" in any style, including coaches, carriages, four-in-hand teams and saddle horses, said to be Kentucky bred and trained single footers.

In October, 1905, a board was elected to draft a charter for the City of Santa Monica. The following year, the charter was ratified at public election and in 1907 approved by the State Legislature. The original townsite had long since overspread its boundaries, particularly on the southeast where it had gone far beyond Pico Boulevard into La Ballona Rancho.

THE INVADERS

Santa Monica's reputation as a placid community was shattered in 1908 when an uninvited guest roared into town: the exhuberant, young movie industry. Vitagraph, Kalem, Essanay all had studios in Santa Monica and it wasn't long before old-time residents watched open-mouthed as the young "whippersnappers" began taking over. The movie makers invaded the beach, backyards and stores to get desired backgrounds, always unannounced. According to one story, one of the town's most respected residents innocently walked out of her front door while a scene (featuring Ben Turpin and Broncho Billy Anderson) was being shot on her lawn. She was told, in no uncertain terms, to get back in the house. "An invasion of mad men," cried a columnist. But the madness ended as abruptly as it had begun. By 1915, the last of the studios had left to join the descent on Hollywood. The only exception was Inceville, founded by Thomas H. Ince in 1913. Fortunately, this western movie set, home of such heroes and heart-throbs as Bill Hart and Dustin Farnam, was too far removed at Santa Inez Canyon to churn the waters down the road.

THE OLDEST MASONRY BUILDING in Santa Monica, and possibly the oldest existing building of any kind in the Bay Area, still stands on Second Street between Broadway and Santa Monica Boulevard. It is believed to have been Santa Monica's first City Hall, built in 1873 (the date is interwoven in the grillwork adorning the roof). Some reports say that its days, pre-City Hall, were spent as a saloon and that "on arrival of the Sunday morning train from Los Angeles, a fresh keg of lager was always tapped for the pleasure seekers." After city officials abandoned it, the building served as a jail, a beer garden (again), a Salvation Army meeting hall, and as part of the first Vitagraph movie studio. In the early days of the automobile it also housed a radiator repair shop and more recently a piano tuner.

89

NATIONAL ACCLAIM

While most roads remained relatively inactive, especially during the "off" season, three did not. San Vicente Boulevard, Ocean Avenue and Wilshire Boulevard (between Santa Monica and the Soldiers Home at Sawtelle) formed a perfect triangle and became a natural racing course for Southern California's young auto enthusiasts. Starting in 1909, and lasting through the teens, the road races boosted Santa Monica's name (and the ire of many residents) from coast to coast. Before World War I, the Vanderbilt Cup and Grand Prize Races were among the most famous in the nation.

AN AUTOMOBILE CHUGS along beach road, north of Santa Monica, on what is now Pacific Coast Highway. Ca 1910.

SANTA MONICA BEACH and palisades, ca 1910. Signs along the road urged passersby to "Patronize the Canyon Bath House." Railroad tracks were removed in 1933.

ON THE BEACH at Santa Monica Canyon, ca 1910. Signs, such as the large one here, were an inexpensive way to promote local development. "Watch Santa Monica Canyon grow," it urged visitors, at the same time boosting the locale as "the most natural point for a wonderful resort . . . destined to become the playground for many thousands of people . . . where ocean and mountains meet." Smaller sign, in right foreground, reads: "Free parking on lot across railroad tracks." Pier in background is the shore end of the Long Wharf.

FISHERMAN'S VILLAGE, a short-lived settlement just north of Potrero Canyon, sprang up on the beach after the Southern Pacific abandoned the Long Wharf. It housed a mix of Russian, Japanese and Spanish anglers who reportedly brought in a carload of fish per day. Ca 1912.

94

SANTA MONICA HIGH SCHOOL, three years after opening in 1912.

SANTA MONICA'S TWO PIERS appear as one, 1916. The smaller Loof Pier was the predecessor of today's Newcomb Pier and held the amusement area. The adjoining Municipal Pier was reconstructed in 1921 when it was widened and extended to 1,640 feet.

96

LOOKING NORTH on Third Street in Santa Monica, ca 1916. The cross street is now Santa Monica Boulevard. City hall (page 67) is seen in upper right corner, fronting Bank of Santa Monica building (shown on page 37).

By legislative act, approved April 10, 1917, the State of California made a grant to the City of Santa Monica, in trust for harbor and other public purposes, of the tidelands and submerged lands within the boundaries of the city and below the mean high tide line. This made the city's waterfront activities possible, including its breakwater (built in 1934) and yacht harbor for which Santa Monicans voted a $690,000 bond issue in 1931—despite the Great Depression.

THE FIRST ISSUE of the Santa Monica Evening Outlook was published by Lemuel T. Fisher from his office at the corner of Third Street and Nevada (Wilshire Boulevard) on October 13, 1875, only months after the city was founded. From the start, the Outlook has been more than a local newspaper reporting community news and growth. Over the years it has led, inspired, even goaded - and has remained an influential force in the city's development. Originally an eight page weekly, it sold for $2.00 per year (subscription price), payable in advance.

The Outlook has had several later homes: on Third Street (below) between Broadway and Santa Monica Boulevard (now a movie theater), at 1245 Fourth Street (where Unity By-the-Sea Church now stands), and its present site at 1540 Third Street.

THE DAILY OUTLOOK
SANTA MONICA

40 CENTS PER MONTH

The Daily Outlook and Los Angeles Express

60 Cents Per Month

DELIVERED TO ANY PART *of* THE CITY

When the Carrier Boys are Willing

Ad from 1902

SANTA MONICA EVENING OUTLOOK

TWO PRE-1920 VIEWS of an early tourist attraction: Castle Rock on the beach north of Santa Monica, mid-way between Sunset and Topanga Boulevards. Regarded as a traffic hazard, the natural landmark was leveled by dynamite. Today, only the smaller rocks remain.

SUFFRAGETTES led Venice's first Fourth of July parade down Windward Avenue, ca 1916.

VENICE CANALS AND SHORELINE from the air, ca 1918. Large inland water area (at west end of the Grand Canal) was the Main Lagoon. Triangular area (right center) was "United States Island," a complex of rental bungalows, accessible only by Venetian bridges, where 25 families could enjoy resort living in a setting of palm trees and flowers. Fronting Altair Canal (now Altair Place), about a third of the bungalows are still in use. The massive breakwater at the end of the pier was constructed when the Venice pier was unable to withstand its first major storm. To salvage the pier, Abbot Kinney hastily ordered the building of the breakwater (advertised as the only private breakwater in the land) around the seaward end. It proved to be another engineering error, as well as a near financial disaster for Kinney. The breakwater began to divert currents in such a way that the beach severely eroded and, by 1915, waterfront homes were being pounded by high tides. Kinney tried unsuccessfully to reverse the damage for more than 15 years. It wasn't until the construction of the Hyperion Outfall Sewer in the '30s that the beaches were restored to their natural state.

*MANY BUNGALOWS on "United States Island"
are still in use today.*

ONLY A PORTION of the Long Wharf remains in this Bay view from the California Avenue incline, ca 1917.

NORTH FROM SANTA MONICA CANYON toward Pacific Palisades and Malibu, ca 1922. The lighthouse on the point, which was the landing site for the Long Wharf, was erected in 1912. The tower and adjoining building served as Life Guard Headquarters for Will Rogers State Beach in later years. When the structure was demolished in November, 1972, the lighthouse was preserved for eventual use on the Pepperdine University campus in Malibu.

SANTA MONICA FROM THE AIR, 1919, shows how southern portion of city was first to develop. Tree-lined street cutting across upper portion of picture is now Wilshire Boulevard.

LOOKING TOWARD SANTA MONICA from the Huntington Palisades, ca 1920. Grasses that grew on the flatlands were harvested as feed for cattle that roamed the area. Note portion of Long Wharf in lower right of photo.

VIEW FROM PACIFIC PALISADES looking toward Malibu shows Inceville (on point in center of photo), one of California's early movie studios. Founded by Thomas H. Ince, pioneer producer (and subject of the William Randolph Hearst yacht scandal in 1924), Inceville was a vast village of sets that stretched around the point into Santa Inez Canyon along what is now Sunset Boulevard. Note large set on mesa above "Jones Bowl." Inceville was destroyed by fire in the early 1920s. Ca 1919.

LOOKING DOWN Rustic Canyon toward the bay, ca 1921. Eucalyptus trees (right background) were planted by Abbot Kinney as an experiment to discover which species would survive in the coastal climate.

THE MAIN ENTRANCE to Santa Monica Canyon, ca 1920.

A GLITTERING TRANSFORMATION

With the dawn of the '20s, following World War I, the rush of people into Southern California turned into a flood. Los Angeles had two booming industries, oil and motion pictures. Venice and Ocean Park were the "fun capitals" of the coast - if not the world. Santa Monica was being reborn with a new civic spirit, seeing itself as the finest residential community in the United States and the most natural center for "refined pleasures." That image was not to last long, however. In 1921, a group of enthusiastic Angelinos formed the All-Year Club to promote the virtues of the Southland. "California has many glories," the ads modestly cried, "but there is only one Santa Monica." The campaign not only brought waves of tourists but a new breed of residents. Overnight, the town lost its staid, provincial and exclusive character. A full-scale amusement pier, one to rival those down the shore, was born - and the beach club era was about to begin. In 1922, ornate clubs started to blossom up and down the beach from Ocean Park to Santa Monica Canyon and by 1923 more than 15 membership organizations were flourishing. The most successful was the Casa Del Mar, which opened in 1924. At its peak its membership approached nearly 2,000 and included such names as composer Rudolph Friml and movie vamp Theda Bara.

FOURTH OF JULY celebration, Santa Monica Bay, 1920.

LIKE A GIANT GLOWWORM, Santa Monica's famous Blue Streak Roller Coaster snaked its way along the brightly lit pier. Ca 1922.

112

THE CASTLE-LIKE Deauville Beach Club, located just north of the Santa Monica Pier on the site of the old North Beach Bath House, 1927. It was torn down in the '50s.

STANDING ROOM ONLY at Ocean Park Beach (Rose Avenue and Ocean Front Walk), 1921. There were days, old-timers recall, when crowds were so thick it was impossible to get near the beach or the pier. The Ocean Park Bath House (right of photo), an orphan on the sand in 1905, now seems almost lost within the surrounding spectacle.

WHERE THE MOUNTAINS
MEET THE SEA
VENICE-OCEAN PARK
SANTA MONICA

PROMOTIONAL PHOTO used to attract visitors to the beach area during the early '20s, a period of extreme migration to Southern California. The setting, climate and economy were all drawing cards - but the glamour and excitement of the fabulous piers received most of the play.

BEACH HOUSES line the road north of Santa Monica Pier, ca 1920. Access to beach from the palisade is famous "99 steps."

BEACH ROAD at Santa Monica Canyon, 1924. Left, same view today. Several of the houses on Mabery Road and Ocean Way may be identified in the earlier photo.

VIEW FROM PALISADES TODAY. The street cross-over has changed but many of the early buildings are still standing.

IN HER ROOM on the second floor of the Ocean View Hotel (far right),
Aimee Simple McPherson changed into her bathing suit to take her legendary
walk into the Pacific – May 18, 1926. (The hotel was recently restored and
reopened as a residence for senior citizens.)

FLEET OF MUNICIPAL BUSES stands "at the ready"
at Hendrick's Corner (Lincoln and Pico Boulevards) to
transport crowds between Santa Monica and
Los Angeles, 1924.

IN 1924, it took some doing to reach Malibu Lake - but the drive was worth it.

PRESTIGEOUS VENICE BEACH, ca 1920, where celebrities stayed and played. Charlie Chaplin was a constant guest at the Waldorf Hotel (right). Mae Murray, Janet Gaynor and Norma Shearer had nearby beach houses. Harold Lloyd and William S. Hart had cottages by the canals. Douglas Fairbanks, Rudolph Valentino, Gloria Swanson, Marie Dressler, Mary Pickford and others made frequent trips to Venice, "the" resort town west of the Rockies. Though some of the glamour has faded, the Waldorf is still in operation - now as the Waldorf Apartments.

114

FACADE of the Waldorf today.

PICTURE-POSTCARD SETTING of the Venice canals during their glory days, 1920-23. Here, residents enjoy boating on what is now the intersection of Main and Windward.

'HERE...IS PACIFIC PALISADES'

In the days following the first World War, the Southern California Conference of the Methodist Episcopal Church had searched for a place to continue the Pacific Coast Chautauqua Camp meetings. That spot was found on a gently sloping mesa overlooking the bay. "Here, indeed, is Pacific Palisades," exclaimed Methodist Pastor Dr. Merle Smith. In May, 1921, the purchase of 1,100 acres of land was made. For financing, an appeal was made to other Protestant Churches which resulted in the sale of Certificates that were later applied to the purchase of lots. On January 14, 1922, the town of Pacific Palisades was founded in a meeting at what is now known as Founders' Oaks. A single tree remains today, set in Founders' Oaks Island on Haverford Avenue.

FOUNDERS' OAKS in Temescal Canyon, ca 1900.

116

THE FIRST Easter Sunday service in Pacific Palisades (looking toward the bay from Peace Hill), 1922.

METHODIST TENT VILLAGE in "Jones Bowl," midway between Temescal Canyon and Sunset Boulevard, was a popular summer playground for early settlers of Pacific Palisades. The "Bowl" is now site of a mobile home park. Ca 1922.

AERIAL VIEW of Pacific
Palisades, 1923. Street cutting
across mesa and down bluff,
between Temescal and Potrero
Canyons, is Via de la Paz.
Winding access road to the
beach, lit by floodlights at
night, was closed in the late
'20s due to slides.

TEMESCAL CANYON
and surrouding mesa from the
Palisades' Inspiration Point,
on the south side of the canyon
(January, 1922). The mesa
required extensive filling and
grading prior to development.
Three giant camps housed the
hundreds of workmen, horses
and equipment necessary for
the job. The Clarence P. Day
Camp, largest of the group,
was near the present
intersection of Radcliffe and
DePauw Streets.

THE "BUSINESS BLOCK," at the corner of Antioch and Swarthmore, housed all of the Palisades' early commercial interests. Fear of earthquakes triggered removal of ornamentation on the roof. Ca 1923. (The first structure in Pacific Palisades was the "Bishop's Cottage," an unimposing little wooden house surrounded by miles of barren land - located on the site of today's Mayfair Market. The cottage originally served as a real estate sales office and was "named" after conversion into a residence for the local Methodist Bishop.)

119

IN 1923, a drive down Wilshire Boulevard in Santa Monica was a quiet drive through the countryside. Here, at what is now the 23rd Street intersection (looking east), towering eucalyptus trees flank the by-way that was destined to become one of the world's most famous and traveled thoroughfares. The following year, 1924, Wilshire was widened. The original plan called for decorative trees, flowers and shrubs, and an alternate succession of historic and artistic arches, obelishks and fountains. Above, Wilshire at 23rd today.

THE PASTORAL "BACK COUNTRY" of Santa Monica Canyon (looking west), ca 1923. Building in right center of photo is the old schoolhouse now on the grounds of Canyon Elementary School.

THE FOLLOWING EIGHT PANELS represent a panoramic view
of the Bay Area, ca 1923. The photos were taken from atop a power
pole at the intersection of Fourth and Marine Streets.

LOOKING TOWARD Culver City past Roselin Plaza.

MOVING WEST, there's a striking increase in the numer of residences.

OVERLOOKING Ballona marshes (now Marina del Rey), Ocean Park, Venice and Playa del Rey.

124

BETWEEN the Venice and Ocean Park Piers, hotels and apartments line the strand.

GATEWAY to the Ocean Park playground.

ACROSS THE BAY, through the haze, Malibu comes into view.

LA MONICA BALLROOM, Santa Monica's giant temple for dancing, stretches skyward from the pier.

SCATTERED HOMES dot the foothills of future communities of Brentwood, Bel Air and Westwood.

129

In 1921, an ambitious young man named Donald Douglas, backed by ten men who put up a total of $15,000, began to make airplanes in Santa Monica. Three years later, the first airmen to circle the globe set forth from Clover Field. Four air cruisers carried the name of Santa Monica around the world and when they returned, 190 days after they had started the flight, 50,000 cheering spectators had gathered to greet them.

130

THE DOUGLAS AIRPLANE FACTORY at
Clover Field where the 'round the world planes
were built, 1924. (Clover Field was named for
Grier Clover, a young aviator who lost his life
in World War I.)

AD from 1924

The Renowned Clover Field—Start and Finishing Point of the History Making Round The
World Flight in the Year 1924

This Field is Now Municipally Owned by the
City of Santa Monica. Sketch is of the Municipal
Golf Course, Flying Field, Round The World
Flight Monument and new Location of the
Famous Douglas Airplane Company Factory

ENTRANCE to the Venice Pier, 1924. In the background, Venice beach and the marshes of the
La Ballona-Marina del Mar (now Marina del Rey) area.

132

THE MIDWAY of the Venice amusement area with its rides, shops and game parlors, 1924. The famous Ship Cafe, hangout for many Hollywood celebrities, is "moored" between the roller coaster rides. Thrills and excitement were just part of Venice's lure - another was that it was one of the only "wet" communities in the Southland during Prohibition.

133

VENICE PIER, looking shoreward down the midway, 1924. Tall structure in center is the Bamboo Slide. Ride in foreground is the Coal Mine. The Ship Cafe (right) was supposedly modeled after Juan Cabrillo's Spanish galleon.

AFTER VENICE REACHED its popularity peak in the early '20s, various celebrations were staged to help promote continued interest in the area. Above, Windward Avenue during Mardi Gras, 1924.

CROWDED VENICE BEACH, 1925. Tall building (left) is the Waldorf Hotel. Sloping roof (right center) tops the cavernous Venice Plunge. Erector set-like structure on the pier is the Flying Circus ride. Max Sennett shot many of his famous bathing beauty scenes on this beach.

FIRE played an important part in the history of the Ocean Park Pier - from major blazes like those of 1912 and 1924 to the smaller ones that plagued it during its final days in the mid-1970s. Here, probably the most disastrous fire of all . . . January 6, 1924.

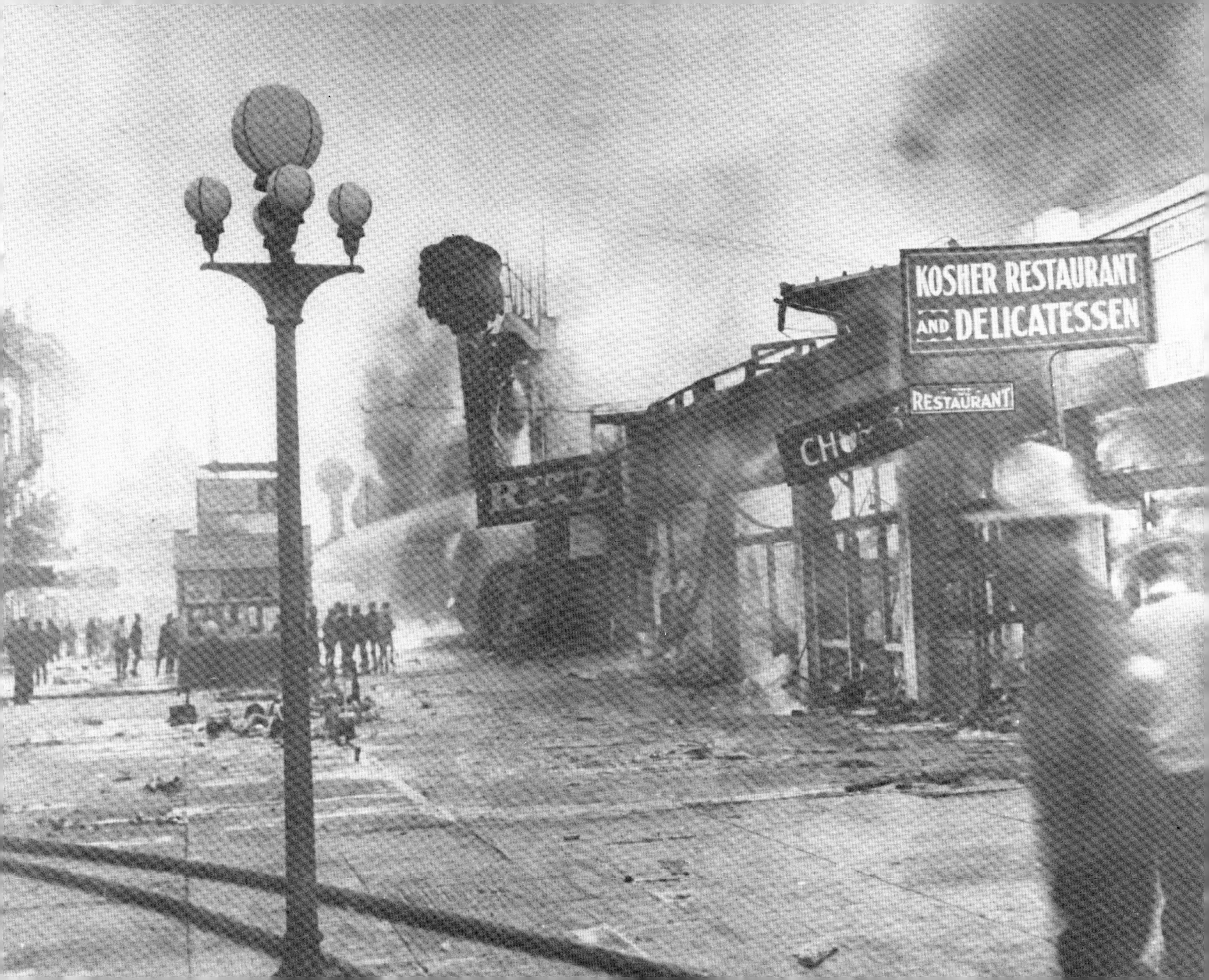
KOSHER RESTAURANT
AND DELICATESSEN
RESTAURANT
RITZ

ADVERTISING, 1924.

140

143

PACIFIC PALISADES ~ SEPT. 1925.

WINDERMERE HOTEL ~ Santa Monica

MERRITT-JONES HOTEL ~ Ocean Park

LOOKING TOWARD Santa Monica from Rose and Main Streets, early '20s.

144

PACIFIC PALISADES - from Peace Hill to the bay, 1925. For many years, Peace Hill was marked by a tall, white wooden cross, illuminated at night and visible for miles. Eventually, the cross was removed and erected on the tower of Pacific Palisades Community Church. (In photo, the large building in right center is The Business Block; the canyon in upper right is Temescal.)

THE TOTEM POLE, located in the northerly end (Inspiration Point) of Palisades Park, was made for J. Walter Todd in 1925 by the Chilkat Thlinger Indian tribe of Sitka, Alaska. Later that year, Mr. Todd presented the giant carving to Santa Monica as a symbol of his love for the city. It has become a landmark.

The La Monica Ball Room
Excels in Beauty and Splendor

SPECTACULAR LIGHTING EFFECTS
FINEST DANCE FLOOR IN AMERICA
5,000 CAN DANCE WITH COMFORT
ROOM FOR 5,000 SPECTATORS

THE LA MONICA BALLROOM on Santa Monica Pier was billed as the largest ballroom in the world (it could accommodate 10,000 persons easily - with room to roam). Inside, with its ornamental carvings, gilt chandeliers, carved ballastrades and upholstered settees, the setting was palatial, reminescent of some exotic far-off land (the vogue in silent movies of the day). Outside, with its stylized Byzantine domed turrets, the building looked strangely fascinating as it "floated" on pilings above the surf - a giant arena from another time and place.

146

SOUTH SIDE of the La Monica Ballroom, 1926. In later years, when its glory days as a dance palace had faded, other attractions such as country-western shows lured customers to the then renamed Santa Monica Ballroom. Ultimately, the building was transformed into a roller rink. After several bouts with fire, it was torn down in 1963.

IN 1924, the La Monica Ballroom was open for dancing at 7:30 pm every night of the year - with afternoon matinees scheduled for 2:30 pm. Loge seating was available around the perimeter of the dance floor for spectators and reservations were necessary. The resident orchestra of 18 musicians was conducted by Don Clark.

148

LA MONICA BALLROOM, largest in the world, lit up the nighttime sky from Santa Monica Pier, 1923.

149

SANTA MONICA PIER and beach just prior to start of construction on the Deauville Club (in parking lot area), 1925.

LOOKING NORTH on Ocean Avenue, 1927. During the '20s, hundreds of cars were often parked along the palisades at dusk to watch the spectacular sunsets.

AS IT DOES TODAY, this grassy oasis-on-the-beach offered visitors in 1926 a comfortable place to relax and play. The park, with its colonnaded arbor, is located just south of Pico Boulevard. The Crystal Beach pier is seen in the background.

TRAFFIC JAM along the beach north of Santa Monica Canyon, 1926. (Some things never change.)

LOOKING DOWN on Sorrento Beach from Palisades Park, 1926. The building in the lower left, long used as a summertime refreshment stand, was torn down in October, 1974. The beach, a favorite with college students, has broadened considerably since the construction of the breakwater in 1934.

THE "HIGHWAY" through Topanga Canyon, 1925. First settled in 1875, the canyon has a rich history dating back as far as 5,000 years when primitive Indian tribes roamed the mountains. (Relics have also been found that indicate activity over 10,000 years ago.) Today, residents of Topanga are continually fighting the "battle of the bulldozer" to protect the natural, rustic beauty of their canyon from subdividers.

153

ADVERTISING

1926

OCEAN PARK

The Unsurpassed All Year

"PLAYGROUND OF THE WEST"

Because the miles of natural silver strand bathing beach

THE MAMMOTH INDOOR

OCEAN PARK PLUNGE

ALWAYS COURTEOUS ATTENDANTS AND EFFICIENT
SWIMMING INSTRUCTORS

THE IDEALLY BEAUTIFUL AND ALLURING

EGYPTIAN
BALLROOM

And innumerable high-class attractions on the

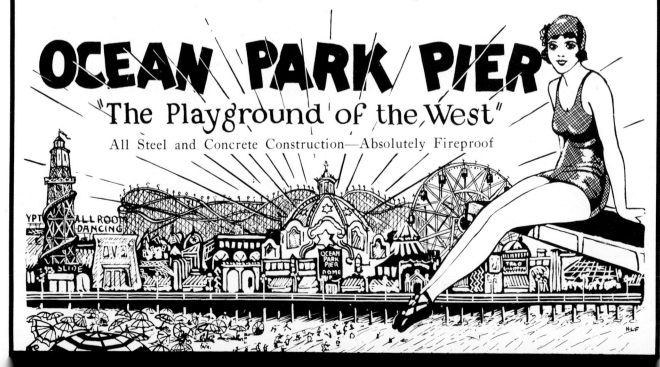

OCEAN PARK PIER
"The Playground of the West"

All Steel and Concrete Construction—Absolutely Fireproof

157

158

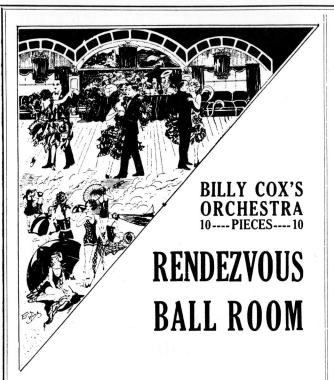

*CRYSTAL BEACH, mid-way between Santa Monica and Ocean
Park Piers, was a popular place to relax - if you could find a
spot. The Crystal Beach Bath House and Plunge, an open-air
attraction located at the foot of Hollister Avenue, was
removed in the '50s.*

LOOKING NORTH to Santa Monica Boulevard on Fourth Street, 1928. With a thriving population of 50,000, Santa Monicans noted, "We are just far enough away from Los Angeles to appreciate her and not close enough to be overwhelmed."

161

Lincoln Junior High School, Santa Monica, 1928. Built in 1898, the building served as the city's high school until 1912 when Santa Monica High opened.

MEMBERS of Santa Monica Bay Telephone Company's outside crew gather near the corner of Colorado and Cloverfield (looking east). A brick manufacturing plant is in the background. May, 1928.

THE ORIGINAL SANTA MONICA Hospital (ca 1926) was established in 1925 by the Lutheran Hospital of Southern California. Through continuing expansion programs, capacity has increased to 324 beds in a facility that now covers three-quarters of a city block.

AERIAL VIEW of Ocean Avenue and Adelaide Drive, ca 1925. Many of the original homes in the area can be identified in the current photo.

SHOTGUN SQUAD of the Santa Monica Police Department, 1927. Photo was taken at Idaho and Ocean Avenue entrance to Palisades Park.

A LEISURELY DRIVE through Santa Monica Canyon in 1927 took sightseers past oak-shaded tents and log cabins.

SANTA MONICA

CANYON

1927

SANTA MONICA
Canyon's business district,
1928.

ADVERTISING, 1928

HENDRICK'S CORNER, Pico and Lincoln Boulevards.

169

HORSEBACK RIDING was a popular diversion in the '20s, particularly in the Bay Area where more saddle horses were available than anywhere else in Southern California (one local stable had more than 300 head of the finest stock in the southwest). Enthusiasts had a wide choice of places to ride. There were endless paths along the foothills, quiet trails among the scenic canyons, deserted stretches on the northerly beaches, even spots within the private estates that bordered the Santa Monica city limits. Active sportsmen were often found participating in matches on polo fields at the Uplifters Ranch and Saddle Club or Will Rogers privately owned estate in Pacific Palisades.

MILES PLAYHOUSE on Lincoln Boulevard in Lincoln Park was named after J. Euclid Miles who, in 1925, willed $20,000 to the city of Santa Monica to build a hall for young people. The playhouse opened in 1929.

ADAMSON BEACH HOUSE on Vacquero Hill, at the mouth of Malibu Creek and adjoining Surfriders State Beach, was designed by architect Stiles Clement in the early '20s for Mrs. Rhoda Adamson, daughter of Frederick and May Rindge. Construction began in 1928 and was completed in 1930. Colorful tiles, designed and made by European craftsmen in Malibu, were used extensively throughout the house and around the grounds on the 13 acre site. Vacquero Hill, one of the last remaining ties to Malibu's historical and cultural heritage, was recently acquired by the State of California.

*THE NORTHWEST CORNER of
Fourth Street and Wilshire Boulevard, 1928.
The complex is still known as "The Medical
Building" although its exterior appearance
was changed during the '60s from Spanish
to contemporary design.*

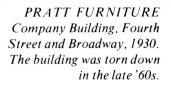

*PRATT FURNITURE
Company Building, Fourth
Street and Broadway, 1930.
The building was torn down
in the late '60s.*

THE LITTLE, ONE ROOM SCHOOLHOUSE on the grounds of Canyon Elementary School in Santa Monica Canyon is said to be the second oldest school building in Los Angeles County. Declared a historical monument in 1965, it was originally built on what is now Sycamore Road in 1894. (The Santa Monica Board of Education raised $2,000 by tax in the district to acquire a site, building and furnishings, and for payment of salary to a teacher for one year at $60 per month.) In 1933, the school was moved to its present site at 421 Entrada Drive. Still in use, it now serves students as a library.

STANDING WITH HER BACK to the bay, in a heart-shaped mound of grass at the foot of Wilshire Boulevard, the statue of Saint Monica watches over the city that bears her name. The sculpture is the work of Eugene Morahan and was placed in Palisades Park in 1935. (The legend of the city's name dates back to 1769 when Spanish soldiers camped at what is now San Vicente Springs, located on the grounds of University High School in West Los Angeles. With the soldiers was Father Juan Crespi, who called the springs Santa Monica because the gentle waters reminded him of the tears of Saint Monica weeping for her wayward son who later became Saint Augustine.

SANTA MONICA

177

ON SANTA MONICA'S *Sorrento Beach,*
surfers stand with their oversize pre-war boards.
Man on right is muscle-builder Vic Tanny.

SURFING *hadn't yet reached boom proportions in 1941 but it still had its followers as shown by this small group gathering*
off the tip of Santa Monica Pier. Large buildings on shore are (l-r) Monica Hotel (formerly the Breakers Club), the
Kabat-Kaiser Institute (formerly the Edgewater Club - demolished in the '50s), and the then Del Mar Club (now Synanon).

178

THE ORIGINAL SAINT JOHN'S HOSPITAL shortly after opening in 1942. Continued expansion has marked the growth of this exceptional facility. The north wing was added in 1953 while the larger south wing opened in 1967. Saint John's is operated by the Sisters of Charity of Leavenworth.

179

SPIRIT
. . . AND GROWTH

Santa Monica Bay's contribution to the war effort was, in part, the filling of tremendous orders from the government and from foreign countries for aircraft. The Douglas Aircraft Company plant, camouflaged almost to invisibility, expanded its output to break all records. The area swarmed with wartime workers. Barrage balloons, designed to help protect against invasion, together with fighter planes hidden in oddly painted hangers, were decorative additions to the local scene. Blackouts and brownouts were part of the nightly program - and the coastal cities were often packed with servicemen on leave.

The Bay Area moved into the post-World War II era with much the same verve that followed World War I. It was the '20s all over again - but without the ballyhoo. New waves of homeseekers descended on the coastal region, more than replacing the Douglas workers who had departed after war production faded. A furious building boom was launched. New homes, new apartments, new commercial structures appeared seemingly overnight. With rents frozen and private homes in constant demand, real estate men did a raging business. It marked the beginning of the most incredible period of progress in the Bay's history.

AT THE TURN OF THE CENTURY, Malibu was virtually an "island" along the coast, having been cut off from its neighbors by Frederick Rindge's policy of isolation. No through roads existed; trespassors were not welcomed. In 1903, as the sole landing point for supplies for his ranch and railroad, Rindge built the original Malibu Pier, located near the mouth of his Malibu Canyon headquarters. Today, on the same site, a new pier stands (above). Construction began in 1942 and was completed in 1946.

SANTA MONICA BEACH, 1951. For years, because of the celebrated residents (including Cary Grant, Darryl F. Zanuck, Mae West, Brian Aherne), elegant homes and lavish parties, this strip of Pacific Coast Highway was known as "Rolls Royce Row." The large estate (center) belonged to Marion Davies. Built for her by William Randolph Hearst in 1928, it cost $7 million and contained 118 rooms and 55 baths. Many rooms, some dating back to the 16th Century, were imported from Europe (extracted bodily from palaces and estates) for reassembly on Santa Monica beach. (Right photo) Today, all that remains of the Davies mansion are the servants quarters, guest house and cabanas (the main house was torn down in 1955). The property now serves as a private beach club.

TWO AERIAL VIEWS from the '50s. (Left) Mid-town Santa Monica. Santa Monica Boulevard cuts vertically through center of photo. (Right) The coastline from Ocean Park to Malibu.

SANTA MONICA MUNICIPAL AUDITORIUM, 1953. Dedicated on October 25, 1921, the auditorium opened with a performance of Gilbert & Sullivan's "The Mikado" by the Los Angeles Opera Company, featuring Lawrence Tibbett. The huge hall was used for community programs until the late 1950s when it was remodeled for the General Electric exhibit and Administrative Offices as part of Pacific Ocean Park (right). It was destroyed by fire on July 12, 1974.

PACIFIC COAST HIGHWAY at Santa Monica Canyon, 1955.

185

SWANS and other tropical birds add to the peaceful setting of Lake Shrine.

SELF-REALIZATION Fellowship Temple, known as Lake Shrine, in Pacific Palisades was dedicated in 1950 by California Lt. Governor Goodwin J. Knight. The open-air temple, distinguished by its striking golden lotus columns, overlooks a two-acre natural lake. Above, the Gandhi World Peace Memorial. Nearby is a bo tree, descendant of 2,600 year old tree in India.

RIPPLING WATER near Topanga Creek Shopping Center in Topanga Canyon. During rainy season, run-off from surrounding mountains often turn creek into a rushing river. Topanga Canyon Boulevard crosses at bridge (top center).

186

THIS WORLD-FAMOUS SPOT, just south of Santa Monica Pier, was noted not only for its exhibitions of strength and agility but for its colorful crowds as well.

MUSCLE BEACH, July 4, 1956

190   *SANTA MONICA MUNICIPAL and Newcomb Piers, mid-1950s.*

EXPANDING AND REMODELING the Ocean Park Pier in the late '50s prior to reopening as Pacific Ocean Park (POP). Until the new amusement center opened, the pier's carnival atmosphere, complete with fun houses and arcades, was the main attraction.

THE EYES OF THE WORLD *turned to Santa Monica Civic Auditorium on April 17, 1961 for Oscar's big night. The annual Academy Awards ceremonies were held in the beach city through 1968 during which time dozens of internationally famous stars, including Elizabeth Taylor, Burt Lancaster, Sidney Poitier, Patricia Neal, Julie Andrews and Shelley Winters stepped on stage to receive the prized golden statuette. Civic Auditorium, built in 1958, is a favorite showplace for a variety of popular attractions.*

PACIFIC OCEAN PARK *offered fun and excitement for everyone visiting the Ocean Park Pier. Featured attractions included international restaurants, a glittering midway, a sky ride and roller coaster, an underwater diving bell, and a jungle ride through an "erupting volcano." 1964.*

192

THIRD STREET, SANTA MONICA, 1963

LOOKING SOUTH from Wilshire Boulevard.

LOOKING NORTH
from near Santa Monica Boulevard.

LOOKING SOUTH
from Santa Monica Boulevard.

LOOKING SOUTH from Broadway.

CONSTRUCTION OF THE MALL BEGINS, 1964

197

A new look for Third Street . . .

THE MALL OPENS, 1965

CHRISTMAS on the Mall, 1969

199

SINCE 1954, Santa Monica has been the "City of the Christmas Story." Each December, local churches participate in the designing and display of nativity scenes depicting, in sequence, events in the life of Christ. More than a dozen 19-foot "mangers" line a two-and-a-half block stretch in Palisades Park from Wilshire Boulevard southward, where visitors may view the scenes either in their cars or on foot. Opening ceremonies are always held the first Monday in December with a "Singing Cross Parade" consisting of 175 carolers from area church youth groups. The parade winds in the park with a concert of carols for the spectators.

MORETON BAY FIG trees (fiscus macrophylla) on La Mesa Drive, just off San Vicente Boulevard in Santa Monica, were planted in the mid-20s. These magnificent evergreens are noted for their gnarled surface rooting.

CALIFORNIA'S STATE TREE, the coral tree (erythrina caffra), is shown to advantage in the parkway dividing Santa Monica's San Vicente Boulevard. A native of South Africa, the coral tree is particularly spectacular when in bloom. In late winter, after most of the leaves have dropped, the spreading branches become a mass of brilliant red-orange flowers. The trees may also be seen in the parkway dividing Olympic Boulevard. The first coral tree in Southern California is said to have been planted on Vacquero Hill in Malibu.

201

FIRST VEHICLES "christen" the last link of the Santa Monica Freeway on Opening Day, 1966, bringing surrounding communities "that much closer" to the Bay Area.

DECORATIVE ART OF THE TIMES

THE CORNER of Ocean Avenue and Wilshire Boulevard in April, 1970. Construction of the Lawrence Welk Plaza (General Telephone Company building and Champagne Towers Apartments) was in its initial stages. The complex dramatically changed the Santa Monica skyline.

THE OLD MISSION-STYLE BUILDING on Fifth Street and Santa Monica Boulevard was originally built as a combination Town Hall and Public Library in 1904. Later, the building served exclusively as the main branch of the Santa Monica Public Library until newer, larger facilities were available in 1965. In the early '70s, it was found structurally unsafe and razed in 1974.

SUCCULENT GARDEN-in Santa Monica's Palisades Park, 1973.

THE TREES

OF

PALISADES PARK

207

SANTA MONICA MUNICIPAL PIER, 1973

THE PIER'S FAMED MERRY-GO-ROUND, built about 1910, was bought by Walter Newcomb in 1935 and brought from the east coast to Santa Monica. One of the country's last hand-carved merry-go-rounds, it features two chariots and 56 colorful, prancing horses.

208

MALIBU'S FAMOUS 'COLONY.'
Silent movie queen Anna Q. Nillson
started the Hollywood trend to this
exclusive strip of beach in 1926. Soon
others followed, paying $75 a month
for leases that had diversion clauses in
the event that liquor was served on the
property, which was owned by May
Rindge, "Queen of the Malibu," who
was dedicated to the strict beliefs of
her late husband, Frederick.
Pepperdine University is seen on the
hillside in the distance.

THE MALIBU CAMPUS of Pepperdine University is built on a mountainous 650-acre site overlooking the Pacific. A four-year, non-denominational Christian college, Pepperdine began classes in September, 1973.

*BEACHFRONT HOUSES HUG Pacific Coast Highway
just south of Topanga Canyon. Nearly 80 homes along a
1.25 mile stretch northward were razed by the state in 1974 to
return the beach, from Coastline Drive past Topanga Beach,
to its natural condition. Development on the palisade
overlooking the area is Sunset Mesa.*

TOPANGA BEACH, 1973

213

THROUGH THE MORNING HAZE, the Santa Monica skyline stands silhouetted against the eastern sky, 1973.

215

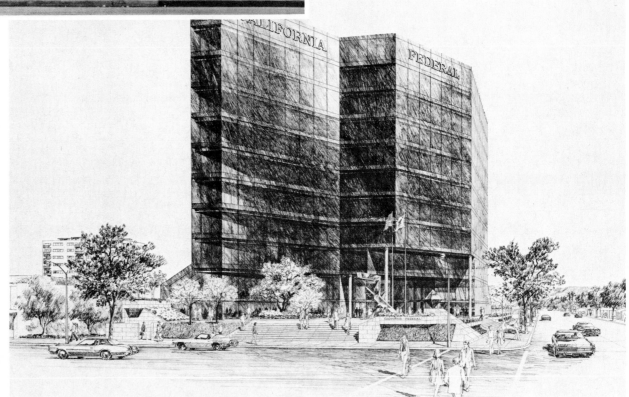

THE NORTHWEST CORNER of Third Street and Wilshire Boulevard in Santa Monica, long a gathering spot for residents and visitors attracted to the international atmosphere of its "shoppes and pubs." A multi-story financial center is planned for the site in the near future.

216

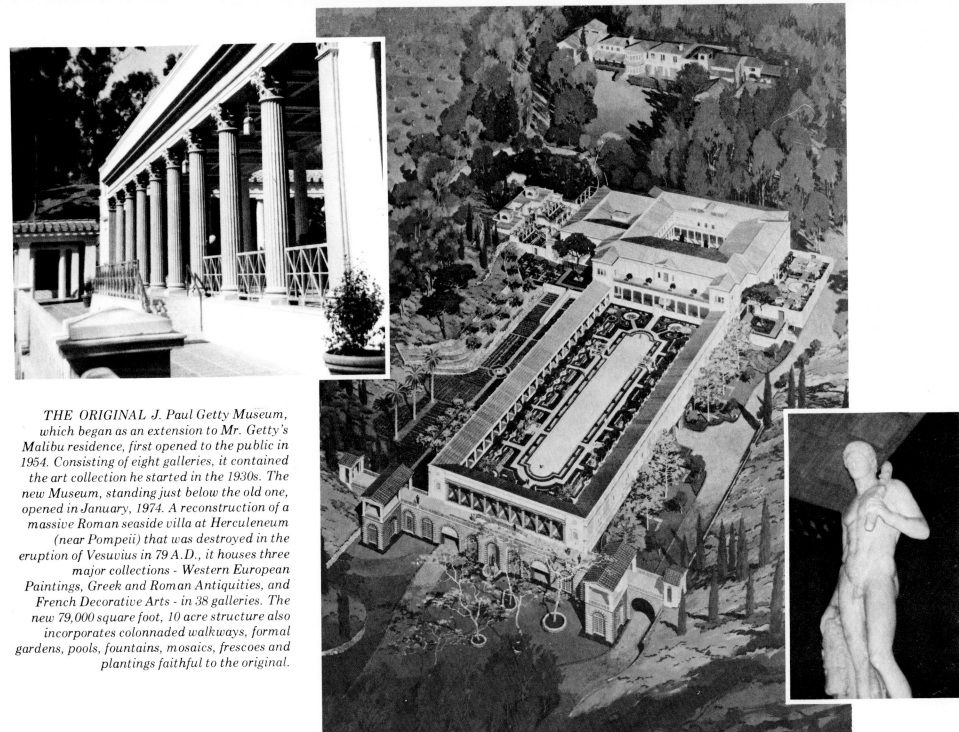

THE ORIGINAL J. Paul Getty Museum, which began as an extension to Mr. Getty's Malibu residence, first opened to the public in 1954. Consisting of eight galleries, it contained the art collection he started in the 1930s. The new Museum, standing just below the old one, opened in January, 1974. A reconstruction of a massive Roman seaside villa at Herculeneum (near Pompeii) that was destroyed in the eruption of Vesuvius in 79 A.D., it houses three major collections - Western European Paintings, Greek and Roman Antiquities, and French Decorative Arts - in 38 galleries. The new 79,000 square foot, 10 acre structure also incorporates colonnaded walkways, formal gardens, pools, fountains, mosaics, frescoes and plantings faithful to the original.

SERRA RETREAT, one of six Franciscan Sanctuaries in the West, rises from Laudamus Hill in Malibu Canyon. The location was originally the site of the proposed Rindge mansion. In the '30s, however, financial problems and the death of Mrs. Rindge halted construction - but not before she had invested more than $500,000 in marble, tile and hand-carved mahogany. In 1941, for $50,000, the Western Providence of the Franciscan Order bought the 26-acre hilltop property, including the half-finished neglected building. Two years later, after erecting a 27-room dormatory and renovating the mansion, the friars opened the sanctuary. The Malibu fire of 1970 destroyed all of Serra Retreat but the Memorial Wing. A new $35,000 facility, consisting of a small chapel, offices and sleeping accomodations for 55 opened in January, 1974.

THE CIRCULAR STONE BENCH, a memorial to Senator Jones, Santa Monica's founder, is located in Palisades Park directly across the street from the site of his estate, Miramar. Here, as the interior inscription reads, "In the evening of his life, John P. Jones used to come each day to watch the sun set over the ocean."

IN HONOR
OF
JOHN P. JONES
FOUNDER OF
SANTA MONICA AND
FOR THIRTY YEARS A
SENATOR OF
THE UNITED STATES
PIONEER OF THE WEST
STATESMAN PHILOSOPHER
FRIEND

ON THE SPOT
HE LOVED SO WELL
THIS MEMORIAL HAS BEEN
ERECTED IN RECOGNITION
OF HIS SERVICES TO
THE CITY OF SANTA MONICA
AND TO
THE NATION

EPILOGUE

Today, the waters of the Bay are as placid, the curve of its shoreline as lovely, and the rise of its bluffs and mountains as imposing as when Juan Cabrillo and his men cast anchor centuries ago.

From the "Bay of Smokes" to a verdant pasture, from a struggling village to an internationally famous playground, from a handful of isolated towns to a sprawling cosmopolitan complex - a thriving panorama so vast not even the Bakers, Jones', Rindges, Kinneys and other giants of the formative years could imagine its equal, even in their finest hour.

Santa Monica Bay, historically rich, looks forward to an even more abundant tomorrow.

SPECIAL THANKS

to the following contributors for their generous assistance and
cooperation in providing historical data and illustrative material...

Dorothy Jones Boden
Tom Carroll (Tom Carroll Photography)
Zola Clearwater
Robert E. Cody (Security Pacific Bank)
Lura Dymond (Westways Magazine)
Bill Ferrell (General Telephone Company)
Sue Gessler (General Telephone Company)
Bill Godbout
Phil Gray (Santa Monica Hospital)
Jack Hageny (Del-Hagen Studio of Photography)
Garry Heath (Garry Heath & Associates)
Larry Lee (Larry Lee Photography)
James Lennon
Ernie Marquez
Dolorez Nariman (Title Insurance & Trust Company)
Cynthia Niemier
Robert Osborne
Angie Otterstrom
Audrey Plant
Sam Porter (Santa Monica Chamber of Commerce)
Frances Roberts (Saint John's Hospital)
George and Grace Shehady
Larry Smith (California Federal Savings & Loan Association)
Harry and Madeline Strangman
Ken Strickfaden
Carl Tegner
Martha Townsend (Santa Monica Public Library)
Sue Waller (J. Paul Getty Museum)
Bill Youngs (Pepperdine University)

INDEX